HIGH NOON
IN AMERICA

January 20, 2009

By: P. Nathaniel Boe, Esq.

authorHOUSE®

AuthorHouse™
1663 Liberty Drive, Suite 200
Bloomington, IN 47403
www.authorhouse.com
Phone: 1-800-839-8640

First published by AuthorHouse 1/16/2009

ISBN: 978-1-4389-4406-7 (e)
ISBN: 978-1-4389-4405-0 (sc)

Library of Congress Control Number: 2009900383

Printed in the United States of America
Bloomington, Indiana

This book is printed on acid-free paper.

DEDICATION

This book is dedicated to **His Excellency President Barack Obama, the 44th President of the United States of America**, a visionary for the ages who has brought "**Change**" to America and the World. The book is also dedicated to each and every Wonderful American who cast his/her vote on **November 4, 2008** to forever change America and the World.

PREFACE

"Change has come to America!!!!!"
President Barack Obama (November 4, 2008)

*A*t **HIGH NOON** on **January 20, 2009,** the Presidential Oath of Office will be officially administered to **His Excellency Barack Obama** as the **44th President of the United States of America.** (See U.S. Constitution, Article II, Section 8 and Amendment XX).

The journey to that momentous and most anticipated occasion of the 21st Century began on January 1, 1863 when the darkness of slavery hanging over the land, the United States of America, gave way to the dawn of a new day as a result of His Excellency **President Abraham Lincoln** issuing the Emancipation Proclamation. Almost two (2) years prior, the civil war had started and pursuant to the President's Commander in Chief powers under the Constitution, President Lincoln took this dramatic action. Because of his bravery, President Lincoln lost his life in 1865.

In the same year President Lincoln lost his life, the United States Congress enacted the 13th Amendment officially ending slavery and it was ratified by two-thirds of the several states. The ratification of the 13th Amendment brought daylight to the United States of America.

But a big cloud has hung over the landscape of the United States since

1865. The clouds of lynching, Jim Crow, segregation, overt and subtle racism have lingered over the years. As the cloud hung low over this beautiful land, there were many voices advocating and praying for a **bright sunlight of change** that would bring equality, justice, opportunity and prosperity to all Americans.

The most eloquent and prominent voice for change during the 100 years removed from 1865 was the **Rev. Dr. Martin Luther King, Jr.,** who stirred the Nation with his "**I have a Dream Speech**" on August 28, 1963 in Washington, DC. His submission to the American People on that memorable day resulted in the passage of the Civil and Voting Rights Acts and many of the other civil liberties the present generation of Americans enjoys.

In Dr. King's submission to the American people, he made one poignant request that the "**American People judge his 3 little children by the content of their character and not by the color of their skin.**" (See Dr. MLK's "I Have a Dream Speech").

Forty–five (45) years later, **on November 4, 2008**, the American People adjudged **His Excellency Barack Obama** not by the color of his skin, but by the content of his character by electing him the **44**[th] **President of the Great United States of America.**

This achievement belongs to all Americans because the People have spoken un-equivocally that America has changed forever!

With this monumental achievement, this book explores the new unlimited opportunities that this "Change" presents to all Americans. This change is a brand new beginning for all Americans. What **We the People** in partnership with our new President do over the next 4 to 8 years will determine if this moment is the beginning of another 100 years of American prosperity. *What will you as an American do with this opportunity called "Change" that has come to America?*

Furthermore, during the final days of the 2008 Presidential Election, President Obama exalted the multitudes stating that if Americans voted to elect him President "they will not only change America, but also change the World."

On that ecstatic November night, at exactly 10:00 PM Chicago Time, as CNN projected **"Sen. Barack Obama Elected the 44th President of the United States,"** time stood still for one second then the world broke into spontaneous celebrations from all four corners of the earth for such a historic verdict. *This book will further explore what will the members of the International community do with this opportunity called "Change" that has come to the world?*

TABLE OF CONTENTS

Chapter One
Smiles of our Forefathers

*P*resident Barack Obama is a visionary leader. He used one word **"Change"** to transform the universe in the most positive way unimaginable. President Obama dubbed his campaign for the American Presidency as an "improbable journey." The best support he needed, he found in his remarkable wife, First Lady Michelle Obama. President and Mrs. Obama are the "change we can believe in" because they represent authentic change. They are an American Original!

This is the magic of America, the intangible ideal that makes America unique and a wonderful place for all mankind especially the down trodden. When one's land is overtaken by senseless civil wars in African, South American, European or Asian countries for a prolonged period of time, America opens it arms to them and provides both a refuge for them and an opportunity to prosper. That's why America is such a wonderful country.

America has experienced tremendous growing pains, but through it all, the ideal of America remained paramount, survived a civil war, end of slavery, women's right to vote, a great depression, 2 World Wars, end of segregation, guarantee of civil and voting rights and avoided a nuclear war for over 60 years.

But through it all, the progress that has been made in America over the past 2 centuries that culminated in the election of His Excellency Barack Obama as the 44th President of the United States has helped all Americans to overcome many of their differences and whatever else that has illed this land. I strongly believe that the act of electing President Barack Obama has not only brought smiles to the living, but it has also brought smiles to our forefathers/ mothers including, but not limited to:

PRESIDENT GEORGE WASHINGTON

The founding fathers of the United States of America must at this moment be very proud of the land for which they fought many centuries ago to establish between the mighty Atlantic and Pacific Oceans. As the folklore story goes, one cool evening, Mr. George Washington decided that Virginia was too warm to drink tea year round. Worse yet, depending on which side of the bed the King woke up in London, he would increase the tax on the tea without consulting with the taxpayers in the colonies in America.

So, one fine day, Mr. Washington put a few good men together called the Founding Fathers. They decided to write a big book of grievances called the Declaration of Independence that the other common tea farmers could not understand. All they knew was that the time to drink tea and pay taxes to London without consultation was over. It was time for a "Change" for Americans to run their own affairs.

After Mr. George Washington and his buddies fired a few shots, the British ran in everywhicheverdirection. In 1776, the USA declared it independence from the British tea drinkers and their tax happy King.

It appears that the Founding Fathers may have thought that by winning the war of independence in 1783, their work was over. No, No! They took several years to write the American Constitution with the main focus being **"We the People ... [are here to enjoy] life, liberty and the pursuit of happiness"** without imported tea from India and paying taxes without consultation to London.

I believe that President Washington must have a big smile on his face because what he and his buddies could not achieve in 1787 during the Constitutional

Convention, the American People concluded on November 4, 2008. The present generation of Americans has written the last chapter of the American Constitution by taking the right steps to reconcile the racial differences of all Americans by electing President Barack Obama. President Washington, your America is a wonderful place and God's blessing to generations yet unborn.

President Abraham Lincoln & Mr. Fredrick Douglas

According to folklore, with tea banned in the United of America, President Abraham Lincoln and Mr. Frederick Douglas, the foremost abolitionist, met at a coffee house in Washington, DC to write the Emancipation Proclamation. So one day, Mr. Douglas asked "when will we put the problem behind us?" President Lincoln asked, "what are you talking about?" Mr. Douglas replied, "Emancipation Proclamation."

Someone in the coffee house overhead the conversation between Douglas and Lincoln about the emancipation and called General Robert E. Lee. Not following the regular protocol of war, General Lee fired his cannon at Fort Sumter in April 1861 and requested the heads of both President Lincoln and Mr. Douglas because he thought that they were about to commit sedition against the Constitution.

President Lincoln sent a letter to General Lee to read the constitution and desist. General Lee took the constitution and read it 20 times but he always had his big thumb on the provision that says "{slavery} shall not be prohibited by the Congress prior to 1808." (See U. S. Constitution, Article I, Section 9 Clause 1)

By misreading the constitution, General Lee plunged the USA into a civil war. As the war lingered, President Lincoln informed Mr. Douglas, I cannot find the draft Emancipation Proclamation and I will need your help to keep this union together.

So one day, President Lincoln sat in his study and hand wrote the text of the Emancipation Proclamation beginning in the summer of 1862. The draft went through several changes. But the text that both President Lincoln and Mr. Douglas agreed upon was issued on January 1, 1863. This move allowed President Lincoln to enlist the freed

African Americans into the Union Army. This was the beginning of the end of General Lee.

The effects of war are never pretty. It is reported that approximately 600,000 Americans lost their lives during the civil war.

Prior to the end of the civil war, General Grant, who commanded the Union Army, once again told General Lee to read the Constitution again. General Lee reread the constitution and found that he was in the 1860s and slavery should have ended as of 1808. When General Lee realized he was wrong, he signed the surrender documents and the civil war was over.

I strongly believe that both President Lincoln and Mr. Douglas must be smiling on the great achievement of electing President Obama that started with their work together some 146 years ago.

Ms. Susan B. Anthony

During the 19th Century, Ms. Susan B. Anthony was a prominent American Civil Rights leader and advocate for women's right to vote. (See Wikipedia). While the 13th Amendment ended slavery and the 15th Amendment granted African Americans the right to vote, women could not vote regardless of race. BUT Ms. Anthony disagreed and put all the wonderful women in the land together and demanded the right to vote.

As part of her legacy, women were granted the right to vote through the 19th Amendment to the Constitution in 1920. In the election of 2008, based on media reports, the women's vote carried President Obama over the finish line. What a smile on Ms. Anthony's face as someone who worked tirelessly with Mr. Douglas to advocate for the freedom of African Americans and women's right to vote.

President Franklin D. Roosevelt

As you may know, throughout human history, fear has caused tremendous problems throughout the world. In his first Inaugural Address, President Franklin D. Roosevelt summoned the sacrifice and will of the American People when he declared **"There is nothing to fear but fear itself."**

The American People decided on November 4, 2008 that there is nothing to fear by reconciling the racial differences of all Americans and finally stated unequivocally **"that all Men {and Women} are Created equal and** {the Americans} **hold these truths to be self evident."**

President Roosevelt must be smiling because the fear that has kept the races apart has been finally removed. President Roosevelt's America is a wonderful place.

President John F. Kennedy

President Kennedy was the visionary for the middle century. He envisioned that America could become the undisputed Superpower of the world if the USA could conquer the Heavens. In the early 1960s, President Kennedy challenged his fellow Americans to put a man on the moon in 10 years. Americans rallied around President Kennedy and put a man on the moon in 7 years.

This is what makes great Presidents. President Kennedy is a great American President because he knew that if he summoned the will, sacrifice and ingenuity of the American People, America never fails.

In 2008, President Obama summoned the greatness of the American People to "Change" this nation forever through unity of all Americans whether Blacks, Whites, Hispanics, Asians, Young or Old. To this great challenge, the American People responded without hesitation by electing President Obama with a supermajority vote.

I strongly believe that President Kennedy is prouder of his America and is looking upon America and the world with a big smile on this face.

Rev. Dr. Martin Luther King, Jr.

It appears that once in every century or half century, God anoints a leader from among the Suffering People to stand up to lead his people to the Promise Land. As in the case of Moses who led God's People out of slavery from Egypt, Moses did not make it to the promise land.

Rev. Dr. Martin Luther King, Jr. like **Moses in the Bible** set the stage for Freedom for his People and summoned the greatness of all his people. During the past century and half, there has been many Great African Americans who stood up for justice and equality for all Americans.

The most eloquent and prominent voice for change during the 100 years removed from 1865 was the Rev. Dr. Martin Luther King, Jr. who stirred the Nation with his "**I Have a Dream Speech**" on August 28, 1963 in Washington, DC. His submission to the American People on that memorable day resulted in the passage of the Civil and Voting Rights Acts and many of the other civil liberties the present generation of Americans enjoys.

In Dr. King's submission to the American people, he made one poignant request that the "***American People judge his 3 little children by the content of their character and not by the color of their skin.***"

Well, Rev. Dr. King, Jr. must be smiling because the American People have answered his **"Sermon on the Mount"** delivered on the Washington Mall in 1963. The American People have judged President Barack Obama "not by the color of his skin, but by the contents of his character." Dr. King's purpose and mission has been realized!!

President Ronald Reagan

In his inaugural address in January 1981, President Ronald Reagan espoused the belief that "America is a Beacon of Hope to the World." He was the cheerleader-in-chief for the American cause that the ideal of America was an experiment in motion. While not intending to fire one shot, it appears that President Reagan bluffed the Soviet Union to spend most of its resources on a military build up for a war Reagan did not intend to fight.

As he rode into the sunset in January 1989, President Reagan quoting a 1630 writer cheered America on one more time and said that he saw "America as a shining city on top of a hill."

President Reagan must be smiling because his America is sure a shinning city on top of hill as the sole superpower and with the election of President Obama, as the First African American Commander in Chief; America is really the "beacon of hope to the world."

In conclusion, I believe that all the preceding generations of great Americans must be smiling for what their posterity has achieved together. I would submit that all Americans would agree that the election of President Obama is the beginning of a new opportunity for all Americans to sacrifice for love of country in order to bequeath a fantastic future to American generations yet unborn.

CHAPTER TWO
CHANGING WASHINGTON DC

*B*asedonempiricalandanecdotal information emanating from Washington DC, the nation's capital, it is a tough city. As President Obama asserted hundreds of times during the campaign, Washington, DC is infested with thousands of lobbyists and representatives of various interests groups. With this knowledge what should President Obama be aware of during his presidency?

President and Mrs. Obama must keep keen eyes on those I would term

"Hijackers of Power." Three examples are discussed below to illustrate how a promising presidency could be lost to the hijackers of power:

Beware of Hijackers of Power

Case Study of President George W. Bush

It appears that President George W. Bush is a good person. Not an evil man from Waco, Texas. Some of my friends strongly disagree with me. But I like President Bush because he had serious challenges in life and he was able to succeed. He managed to get elected two times as President of the United States.

Unlike President Bush, his Vice President, VP Dick Cheney never smiles, projects an unfriendly image and demonizes anyone who disagrees with him.

President Bush on the other hand seems approachable and pragmatic.

President Bush knew or should have known that VP Dick Cheney would try to hijack his presidency when Dick Cheney looked out upon the landscape of America and saw all the other 290 Million fellow Americans and determined that no other person was qualified so Dick Cheney chose himself to be the Vice President to President Bush.

Apparently, what President Bush did not know was that a neo-conservative group based in Washington, DC had already concocted a plan to hijack his presidency. It appears from what unfolded during the past 8 years that the neo-conservatives used the tragedy of September 11, 2001 to take over the

Bush's administration and run it into the ground.

As part of the neo-conservatives' playbook, any voice that disagreed with the agenda they foisted upon the American people, were labeled as "Anti-American" or "Cut and Run." This strategy worked well because, President Bush himself could not disagree with his own team because he would have also been declared "Anti-American" by the neo-conservatives.

Additionally, the hijackers of power believed that no regulation was necessary, especially regulation of the financial markets. I would assume that the hijackers of power may have told President Bush that if he proposed regulating the financial markets, the neo-conservatives were ready to brand him "anti-American, anti-capitalism" and then move to impeach him.

Well, the end result of these actions by the neo-conservatives and inaction by President Bush is an economic implosion of historic proportions. President Bush and his administration's inaction or as others call it "sleeping at the wheels" has cost ordinary Americans trillions of dollars in the form of loss of home and stock equity values.

As President Bush ends his presidency at **High Noon on January 20, 2009,** he will leave office with approval ratings hovering around 25%.

To add insult to injury, the same neo-conservatives who hijacked President Bush's administration and imploded the economy, all sit on television shows and pretend that President Bush is solely responsible for what has happened. Or they make the silly arguments that all the problems predated the Bush administration as a way of obfuscating the mess they have created. No child born yesterday will accept such nonsensical arguments.

It seems that the neo-conservatives responsible for the failures of the Bush Administration may have all abandoned President Bush and are now calling him a "big spending conservative."

CASE STUDY OF PRESIDENT ELLEN JOHNSON SIRLEAF OF THE REPUBLIC OF LIBERIA

The first elected Female President of the Republic of Liberia and the first on the Continent of Africa Her Excellency Madam Ellen Johnson Sirleaf came to power on January 16, 2006 with great promise for success. I strongly support President Johnson Sirleaf because she really wants to change the way business is done in Monrovia. As the world knows, corruption led to Liberia's underdevelopment for almost 133 years and eventually plunged the country into 25 years of instability and 14 years of senseless civil wars. The civil wars resulted in the death of over 250,000 Liberians representing 10% of the population.

In her inaugural address in 2006, President Johnson Sirleaf declared **"corruption as the number 1 enemy of Liberia"** and that she and her administration would work tirelessly to combat corruption.

Well, it appears that the criminal corruption syndicates in Liberia, like the lobbyists in Washington, DC, wasted no time and went to work to put key persons in positions of power in President Johnson Sirleaf's administration. While the President still maintains good intentions for the Liberian people, it appears that the corruption syndicates may have taken over her government.

According to news media reports, President Johnson Sirleaf recently lamented that the "Liberian people have not felt development" and that a "3 year learning period was over" for her government officials and that it was time to go to work for the Liberian People. In a recent interview with the Liberian media, it is reported that President Sirleaf is "shocked" at the magnitude of corruption in government.

President Johnson Sirleaf needs Liberians and the international community's continued support to fight and win the war on corruption in Liberia.

CASE STUDY OF THE AMERICAN FEDERAL BUREAUCRACY

Most bureaucrats are killers of progress. The American Federal Bureaucracy is considered as the unofficial 4th branch of government. Because of the way the Federal appropriations process works, when a President supports a bill that Congress approves and is signed into law, most of the money is spent through the Federal procurement process.

This process usually takes 2 years to obligate and another 2 years to spend the funds. If the bureaucrats decide to kill a program, they can drag their feet for 2 years or more doing planning or, pursuant to their rulemaking powers, writing and re-writing the implementing regulations and then another 2 years to obligate and 2 years to spend the funds. Now, its six years and the money is still not spent and the project could be put on the shelf for new priorities or the priorities of a new administration.

How does President Obama guard against this rather unfortunate possibility?

President Obama's strategy should be to bring the bureaucrats on board as members of his team. If he and his cabinet manage the bureaucracy efficiently it can be an asset to his administration especially if the bureaucrats sense that President Obma's administration values their work and brings them on board as members of "Team Obama." As the old saying goes, it is good to keep your friends close, but it is better to keep your enemies closer.

In conclusion, the challenge for President Obama is how to avoid his presidency from being hijacked by the Washington Elite, Lobbyists, Special Interests and those who are hungry for presidential power but were not elected by the American People. All of these people and/or groups can be referred to as Sharks in Washington, DC.

I believe these sharks are waiting to do to President Obama what Dick Cheney and the neo-conservatives on the one hand did to President Bush or what the criminal corruption syndicates in Liberia are doing to President Johnson Sirleaf. Or what the bureaucrats could do to the Obama Administration.

In the final analysis, it is my humble submission that President Obama and First Lady Michelle Obama must be very vigilant not to allow the Washington sharks to hijack the Obama Presidency.

CHAPTER THREE
ECONOMIC RECOVERY

*A*t this moment in history, the last quarter of 2008, all the indicators of American Prosperity are pointing in a downward direction.

Many books recently published in the United States are preaching the partial eulogy of the United States of America. Notable among them are the "Post American World" by Mr. Fareed Zakaria and "End of Prosperity" by Mr. Arthur Laffer made famous by the Laffer curve during the Reagan years. The author of Post American World has been rewarded handsomely with his own television show.

These books and many others postulate that American domination of world affairs because of its great economic powers is approaching its end, and we must take our money and place them in shoe boxes, under our mattresses and that China is going to be the next Superpower.

Compounding the forecast of a bleak future for the United States are (1) numerous enemies abroad including those who attacked us on September 11, 2001, (2) America's entanglement in Iraq due to untenable evidence, (3) the decline in American individuals' wealth due to the precipitous decline in home and stock values that are down by 50% since the beginning of the summer of 2008, (4) the more than $10 Trillion Dollars of debt America owes, (5) the approximately $500 Billion Dollars annual budget deficit spending, (6) America's crumbling infrastructure of roads, bridges, railroads and electricity grids and (7) export of $700 Billion annually of America's wealth to nations whose leaders and/or citizens treat the USA with disdain.

Current commentators often cite these statistics to argue that the United States is on a downward spiral to the dust bin of history.

These facts are the reality of our times, <u>BUT,</u> I strongly disagree with the mindset of exclusively focusing on the negative aspects of America's wellbeing and only seeing the cup as half full.

I believe that "America is a Wonderful Country." I believe that America's Cup is almost full at approximately seventy-five percent (75%) full. This assertion is supported by the fact that over eighty-(80) percent of Americans are employed, homeownership is at an all time high.

In addition, the American People have always been the masters of their own destiny and prosperity. That keeps me excited about the continued prosperity of the United States of America for the next 100 years.

This excitement is underpinned by the American People's decision to enter into a New Contract with a future destiny that promises prosperity and greatness that America has never experienced before. The world witnessed finalization of this new contract by electing on November 4, 2008 His Excellency **Barack Obama** as the next **President of the United States of America**.

If President Barack Obama could make this improbable journey to the American Presidency, the American People with their new leadership is certain to turn today's hardships of foreclosures and loss of stock values into tomorrow's opportunities and great prosperity.

At **High Noon on January 20, 2009**, millions of Americans will gather in the Nation's Capital, Washington, DC, to be witnesses to a fantastic history. All Americans will have the **"Audacity to Hope"** again believing that anything is possible in this great land called America.

Inadequate Government Responses to Stop the Economic Implosion

As the housing and stock markets, the barometers of middle class wealth in the United States, began imploding in 2008, the Executive Branch and Congress of the United States worked together by taking certain emergency actions to stop the cascading implosion of the American economic system.

The first step was a stimulus package that sent checks to Americans hoping that the expenditure of approximately $150 Billion Dollars would spur consumer demand. The backers of this package argued that this act would bring supply and demand into equilibrium. This gesture did not stop the mounting home foreclosures.

As banking institutions began to fail during the fall of 2008, at the request of President Bush, the Congress approved a $700 Billion Dollars bailout for financial institutions. The concept was that the Federal government would buy the banks' toxic assets (meaning worthless assets) hoping that the banks would use the money to stimulate the credit market that had become static. In exchange for the investment, the Federal Government would have an ownership interest in the banks.

This author and many others opposed this approach because it did not make sense for taxpayers to buy worthless assets. I and many others offered alternatives that were later adopted calling for the Federal Government to provide a line of credit to the banks and in exchange receive preferred stocks in the financial institutions.

This approach has not been successful so far because the money went to the bankers and it appears that they are not making the money available to the American People to invest in the economy.

It appears that the U. S. is experiencing capital flight in that the banks are continuing to finance highly profitable projects outside the United States of America and are giving huge bonuses to fleeing bank executives.

As foreclosures continued to mount across the land and millions of Americans continue to loose their jobs, the country is facing a scarcity of investment capital, in issue is how can the American People help our new President to restore prosperity to the United States of America and **Prevent a Depression?**

$1 Trillion Dollars Community Investment Revolving Fund

Using President Obama's effective internet fundraising strategy, each community in the United States should set up a Community Investment Fund ("CIF"). This investment opportunity should be open to all Americans especially to all the residents of each community. Each community could set up the fund at its local bank or credit union. If the community does not have a bank, the CIF should sponsor its own community bank.

President Barack Obama should call upon the American People for **"all Americans to sacrifice now to avert a depression."** It would be prudent for Americans to adopt a strategy whereby each community investor will obligate himself/herself to invest the 1st income for the first hour of work each pay period. At a minimum each investor should commit the 1st $7.00 he/she makes each pay period for a total of $14.00 per month per investor. For those Americans who make higher hourly rates, they should make the same investment commitment or sacrifice.

For example, if a community has 25,000 residents with the average monthly investment of $20.00, the community's monthly investment could be $500,000.00 or **$6,000,000.00** per year. This could be one of the most effective ways President Obama could continue to excite all Americans to help the country come out of the current economic implosion that Americans are experiencing.

The Federal Government's role could be to establish a $1 Trillion Dollars Community Investment Revolving Fund ("CIRF"). The communities could leverage their capital by getting a line of credit from the CIRF for specific community investment projects.

This strategy puts money directly in the hands of Americans to create jobs right away through increased business activities. This will result in the redevelopment of communities throughout the lengths and breath of the United States.

Investment Strategies for American Communities

One of the main focuses of the CIFs should be the acquisition and/or purchase of all vacant properties, lands, foreclosure properties, abandoned properties (residential/ commercial) and all other properties in the community that have been on the market for three-(3) months or more.

The CIF's real estate division or through partnership with community based real estate companies should reposition each property for the market either as rental property or resell it to community residents who are willing to put in some sweat equity in order to keep the prices of the properties reasonable.

As a strong capitalist, I do not believe that the CIFs should replace market forces, but supplement the work of the market. Another main focus of the CIFs is to prevent neighborhood blight, decline in property values because of "for sale" signs all over the neighborhood, and assist police to minimize crime by providing the resources to help the police to fight crimes in each community.

The CIFs would access their lines of credit at the CIRF for its transactions on as needed basis. Once a transaction is completed, the CIRF will be reimbursed at the closing of each real estate transaction to ensure that the CIRF stays liquid and funds are available for other future transactions. The CIRF will resolve the scarcity of investment capital in inner cities and rural parts of America instantly.

More importantly, the bailout that was given to the financial institutions does not guarantee that those American communities that do not have access to capital will automatically have investment capital available to revitalize those communities and create jobs for the millions of Americans who are hard to employ, hard to reach, train and motivate.

With President Obama's overwhelming and historic victory, if he were to call on the American People to sacrifice their 1st income each pay period, the response will be overwhelming. Because this will not be money taken from paychecks in the form of taxes, these investments should be treated like non-taxable deferred compensation and zero tax on the principal and capital gains. This will encourage investment directly in all American communities.

From an aggregate economic analysis standpoint, let's assume a U. S. workforce or investors pool of 150 Million with an average hourly wage of $20.00. This could translate into an investment of $40.00 per month per investor. Over a period of eight-(8) years, the American People could invest approximately $1.2 Trillion Dollars to match the $1Trillion Dollars of government line of credit.

JOB CREATION STRATEGIES IN AMERICAN COMMUNITIES

How do we turn these investments into jobs for our fellow Americans?

The CIFs should incubate businesses in their communities and give the right of first refusal to the businesses located in the community to perform all the work originating in the community. This will create jobs right away. This assumes that we have community residents who desire to work on the revitalization of each community. This is not a job training program; but this will be an employment program to create jobs in the communities right away.

Once a community resident has a job, he/she could go through a readiness program to qualify for home ownership. The CIF will assist the community resident to access all the programs available to assist them to have a successful and enjoyable working experience. On top of job availability in American communities, home ownership will blossom without the sub prime mess.

Change and prosperity will be at hand again for all Americans because community investors will realize gains from their investments without taxation.

The foregoing strategies are in addition to any plans already on the table to fix bridges, high-ways, roads, railroads and other infrastructure. We should not fix the infrastructure around the communities and leave the communities untouched for another 50 years.

RE-INDUSTRIALIZATION OF AMERICA

As a staunch advocate for the Republic of Liberia to become a manufacturing powerhouse in West Africa, I have fear in my heart that the Great United States of America will one day become a non-manufacturing nation. It is good to have unimpeded international trade as long as the American people have the capacity and facilities to manufacture what it needs in times of trouble.

In *Miracle on the Atlantic Coast, How to Transform Liberia into a Prosperous Country*, I used a terrible hypothetical to dramatize Liberia's lack of self-sufficiency in food production. While that exact scenario may not play out in the United States because of its developed status, but the U.S.A is on the verge of loosing its manufacturing base to our overseas friends.

For America, let's assume there is a war between India and China for a period of three-(3) years and their manufacturing capacities are disrupted. Therefore, 80% of the trade between those countries and the USA disappears. This could cause a serious hardship for the American consumers.

Therefore, as part of the economic recovery plan during President Obma's Administration, the USA should adopt a new manufacturing policy. The USA should provide grants to manufacturers plus a ten year tax holiday renewable for another ten years. These are the same or similar incentives that America's competitors provide to American companies.

This will allow American companies to come home and manufacture right here at home. And provide good paying jobs to Americans.

Chapter Four
God & Country in America

S ome sections of this chapter is an edited version of a subsection of Chapter 4 "New Foundation for Liberia" in my 2007 book titled **Miracle on the Atlantic Coast, How to transform Liberia into a Peaceful and Prosperous Country**. I am re-printing it here to capture the essence of the American experience.

In my 24 years in the United States of America, it appears that the nation is moving further away from God.

It is my fervent prayer that Americans will put God first and back in the center of each American's everyday life. I believe that America may be losing its way from the time of its foundation because America was founded on the reverence of God. The evidence of God being the bedrock of the American democracy is chronicled in *"America's God and Country, Encyclopedia of Quotations"* by Williams J. Federer.

In order for America to continue to be the greatest country on earth for several more centuries, Americans must practice the reverence of God both at home and in their public lives. I strongly believe that Americans must make God the central 1st Pillar in the change that has come to America.

As part of the President Obama's "Change", the American People should restore prayers in public schools and offer Bible classes to our children as a way of grounding our posterity in Christian beliefs and reverence for God. For those who run majority non-Christian institutions, they should also pray to God for his Devine Guidance for the United States of America.

STOPPING BLACK ON BLACK CRIME

The African American community in the United States of America is a very religious community. Most of its prominent leaders are from the religious community.

As chronicled in many books delineating the African American experiences in the United States of America, the history is very difficult to read and even fathom what was wrongfully done to African Americans. (See African American Mosaic, Library of Congress).

Rev. Dr. MLK, Jr. made the case for the African Americans and on his shoulders; African Americans have been lifted to the highest height in American society. This includes the election and inauguration of President Barack Obama and Madam Michelle Obama becoming the First Lady of the United States of America.

President Barack Obama and First Lady Michelle Obama are African Americans who represent the change longed for by African Americans for centuries. American icons like the Rev. Jesse Jackson, Sr. and Madam Oprah Winfrey wept with joy on November

4, 2008 because of this breathtaking achievement in American history.

The challenge for all Americans is what will African Americans do with this change that has come to America? I believe that one of the most vexing issues in the African American community that the American leadership has not addressed is how to **stop the Black on Black Crime** in the United States of America.

President Obama has announced the first strategy. That is for African American males to be fathers to their children by providing the male leadership needed in African American families/homes and communities.

The second strategy is for African American males to begin to eliminate anger from their system. And replace it with positive energy of self love and love for their neighbor. As President Obama characterized his campaign, this is an improbable journey. This will be very difficult because of the tremendous sufferings African Americans and their fore bearers experienced in the United States of America over a period of 500 years.

But I submit that with the election of President Obama, the Americans have reached a point of irreversible reconciliation. As part of this reconciliation, the Congress of the United States of America should pass an Act officially apologizing to African Americans for slavery.

My pastor emeritus Rev. D. Jeremiah A. Wright, Jr. was preaching one day about the sorrows of slavery and the joy of apology and what he said from the following passages are directly applicable to the American situation. He referenced the Books of Exodus and Acts of the Holy Bible:

- **Exodus Chapters 1-17 and Acts Chapter 16** discuss the **"Sorrow of Slavery"** and the sadness, tragedy and destruction that African Americans have experienced over the past 500 years demonstrate the sorrow of slavery that left a bad taste in everybody's mouth.

- On the other hand, **Exodus Chapters 1-17, Acts Chapter 16 and Job Chapter 41** discuss the **"Joy of Apology"** in that those who have done wrong publicly recognize their wrongs and apologize, and such genuine apologies bring joy and renewal to the People.

I believe that the election of President Obama has started renewal in the African American community. In order for this renewal to be meaningful to all African Americans, the Government of the United States should support two strategies that will reverse the current conditions of many African Americans:

Establish an Education Trust Fund for African Americans

So that any African American male/female who graduates from High school will have 100% free college education opportunity available to him/her. This program should be established for a generation. I believe that within that timeframe, one of the current hindrances to African American advancement will be resolved.

Transform Money Spent on Jailing African American into Business Grants

Under this approach, the various states and the Federal Government should bundle 25% then 50% of the aggregate funds they spend on jailing African Americans into an Early Childhood Education and Business Development Revolving Fund. The increased support for early childhood education will enhance the success ratio for African Americans.

In addition, when an African American graduates from college, he/she would have the funding needed to establish a business. Or if he/she joins the workforce, the funds would be available to him/her for down payment on his/her first home. If the home were sold the revolving fund would be reimbursed the amount of the grant. But if the home is sold and the proceeds used to purchase another home, there will be no reimbursement and any capital gains should be tax-free. Finally, a home equity line of credit would be available to be used establish businesses.

Many stories I have heard from the media purport that on the average, some states or Federal government spend approximately $40,000.00 a year to keep one African American locked up in prison. Most inmates spend an average of 5 to 10 years in jail. For the foregoing strategy, if each state took 2 years prison funding for each inmate, that would equal $80,000.00. This means that each African American who makes it though college could have a grant of $80,000.00 waiting for him/her after graduation. The net effect is that the government would save $320,000.00 per inmate for not jailing an African American for the average period of 10 years.

This strategy will be a preventative approach to resolving a systemic problem. This will provide hope to millions of Americans that there is opportunity on the horizon and all they have to do is to complete their college education.

This strategy will not replace the criminal justice system in that there will be certain hardened criminals, recidivists or individuals that commit heinous crimes that must be removed from the general population to protect the health, safety and well being of the general public.

Nationwide African American Young Males Mentoring Program

When ordinary citizens decide to solve a problem, they can do extraordinary things. That's why all Americans need to get involved to reverse the misfortunes of African American males in the United States of America. In an effort to start this journey of renewal for African American males, my Pastor, Rev. Otis Moss, III, recently introduced a movement for all the men of the Church to volunteer to be mentors to the young boys in the Church who are living with single mothers. This strategy is based on the Biblical story of Joseph where an angel appeared to Joseph and informed him that he would be the Father to a boy son called Jesus to be born to Mary. God wanted for Joseph to be the father to God's son, Jesus, although Jesus was not Joseph's biological son. God wanted for Joseph to teach Jesus to grow up to be a good man.

All the Churches and community organizations in America should adopt this strategy if they are not already doing so because this will be an early intervention that could save thousands if not millions of young African American males. Churches must be in the forefront of this change that African Americas need for wholesome growth and development.

CHAPTER FIVE
CHANGING AFRICA
& THE WORLD

On January 20, 2009, all 7 Billion People on the face of the earth would like to be in Washington DC to be witnesses to the fantastic history of the inauguration of President Barack Obama. All of us will not be in DC, but the World will once again come to a standstill at that magic moment.

Outside of the United States of America, the One Billion Africans living south of the Sahara will be hurdled around their radios and television sets with tremendous anticipation.

As someone who is in constant contact with my family and friends in the Republic, it appears that Billions of people around the world are reposing their hopes for survival and change for a better future in President Obama.

Therefore, this chapter focuses how President Obama can have the most positive impact in the shortest possible time on the desperate situations existing in Africa and elsewhere in the world?

I believe that President Obama will not only change America positively, but he can also positively change Africa and the world

CHANGING AFRICA

In the past One Thousand (1000) years, the mother continent, Africa, has endured all the worst sufferings that mankind can unleash unto itself. Beginning with the plagues, internal wars between the various peoples of Africa, the Arab invasion, the western slave trade, the division of Africa as colonies in 1884, the battles of the Cold War in Africa, corruption by many thoughtless African despots and the resulting Civil Wars have all contributed to the total devastation of the Continent of Africa.

In order to bring Africa back from the brink of total destruction and underdevelopment for another 1000 years, Africa was included in the 15 year United Nations' ("UN") plan called

Goals of the Millennium Declaration ("MD") to be reached by 2015.

Furthermore, during the Group of 8 ("G8") Summit in Gleneagles, England, in 1995, the leaders issued the Gleneagles Communiqué ("GC") signed by all the leaders of the G8 nations at the end of the Summit. The GC indicated that it is finally Africa's time for renaissance, renewal, growth and development (See Gleneagles Communiqué).

I believe that all Africans who have suffered through the centuries especially the past several decades at the hands of their own non-thinking leaders certainly welcomed the historic declarations and good intentions exhibited in the pronouncements by the G8 leaders!

The G8 acknowledged at Gleneagles that "**Africa is the only continent not on track to meet any of the Goals of the Millennium Declaration by 2015.**"

In light of the stark concern, the G8 decided to provide an additional $25 Billion annually for a total of $50 Billion for development financing for Africa to assist Africa to meet the Millennium Goals within the remaining ten (10) years (See Paragraphs 24 to 28 of GC).

The United States of America is the leading Nation within the G8. While it is not unusual for world leaders to pronounce lofty goals at summits, everyone thought that the G8 pronouncements would be different. Much has not been written or mentioned in the news media about the results of those declarations.

Even prior to the G8 promises in England in 2005, the United States of America has at least since WWII provided annual economic development funds for Africa. The United States Congress provides the funding known as the **Economic Support Funds to Africa and the Development Fund for Africa**. The United States also provides funding for Africa's development through tri-lateral institutions.

Despite all of these funding that have been poured into Africa, the plight of the ordinary Peoples of Africa remain unchanged and is worse for most Africans especially south of the Sahara. In light of Africa's plight and the billions of U. S. taxpayers' dollars that have been squandered by despotic African leaders over the past several decades, in issue is how can President Obama positively change Africa?

U. S. ROLE IN THE ECONOMIC DEVELOPMENT OF AFRICA

As a start, President Barack Obama should separate the development funds for Africa from funding for security and social programs. The State Department and U. S. Agency for International Development ("USAID") should continue to execute those non-economic development programs including the peace and security, healthcare and education.

President Obama should move Africa's economic development agendas from all the various U. S. government agencies and consolidate them into a **Whitehouse Office of Economic**

Development for Africa. President Obama should appoint a **White House Chief Development Officer ("CDO") for Africa** who will run this office. This person should be a Special Assistant to the President. The CDO will be responsible for the development of non- active oil producing African countries south of the Sahara.

Once the White House Office of Economic Development for Africa is established via executive order, the President should establish the **Africa Economic Development Revolving Fund.** The corpus of the revolving fund should be from the consolidation of the various programs from various cabinet departments and other U. S. Government agencies.

Also, the President should request Congressional funding up to **$25 Billion Dollars per year**. Over an eight year period, the fund will have a **total endowment of approximately $200 Billion Dollars.**

U. S. Implementation of African Development

For only the purposes of this strategy, the U.S. should divide Sub-Sahara Africa into four (4) development zones or quadrants, consisting of West Africa, Central Africa, East Africa and Southern Africa. Each zone should consist of a maximum of twelve-(12) countries, and the U.S. should rotate the funds among the four zones on a yearly basis.

The U.S. should make available the entire $25,000,000,000.00 per year to only the twelve countries in a zone for that year by using its current or revised foreign aid formula to distribute the funds among the twelve countries. This focused expenditure of the development fund for Africa is the best way to improve the lives of the ordinary citizens of the various Sub-Sahara African countries.

The economic development fund should never be transferred directly to the beneficiary country's government. Instead, the funds should be transferred through American companies whose officers, officials and employees are subject to American law.

By way of example, let's assume that in 2010, the U.S. designates the West Africa zone in which Liberia is included to receive the entire $25,000,000,000.00. Based on the U.S. foreign aid formula,

Liberia receives Two Billion Dollars ($2,000,000,000.00). In that event, the U.S. should require Liberia to submit a detailed plan of its needs to the **White House Chief Development Officer for Africa**.

The plan should outline the project(s) that are critical to Liberia's development over the next four-(4) years. If Liberia proposes that it needs three-(3) hydroelectric plants to supply electricity, a network of highways, schools and hospitals, airports, railroads, development of tourism, factories to manufacture 10% of it iron ore into steel, rubber cement and wood production, the WH CDO for Africa will work with Liberia to finalize the plan.

The next steps include the CDO soliciting American private sector firms that are willing to engage in Build Operate Turnover ("BOT") projects in Liberia. The private sector companies will either be investors in the projects or project managers for the American and Liberian parties.

The selected U.S. companies will then go to Liberia and select and subcontract with local Liberian owned businesses (meaning Liberian citizen(s) own or control 51% or more of the businesses) to help undertake and complete the various development projects. The beauty of this strategy is that not one dime of American economic development fund will be spent in Liberia without the American companies' representatives and the WH CDO staff personally inspecting the project and certifying that the work has been completed satisfactorily before any American money is released.

The benefits of this strategy include the following:

First, this method of investing American money in Africa will directly and indirectly create millions of new jobs for Americans in the 21st Century. The U.S. companies that contract with the U.S. government will be directly subject to the Foreign Corrupt Practices Act, <u>15 U.S.C. §78m(b) et seq.,</u> (hereinafter, "ACT"). A violation of this Act by American Government employees, consultants and private sector contactors will be prosecuted in the U.S. under this Act.

An individual or firm that bribes a foreign official or engages in any corrupt acts and found guilty under the Act could serve up to ten (10) years in prison in the USA and/or suffer up to Two Million Dollars ($2,000,000.00) in fines.

Second, the ordinary citizens of the various African countries in the four zones will personally see, taste and feel American development funding in action and help to improve Africans' living standards. As African's living standards improve, they will become a market for American goods and services in the 21st Century and beyond. This means the U.S. will have a prime and favorable position with about One Billion Africans south of the Sahara.

The United States is revered in Europe and Japan because the U.S. helped rebuild them after WWII and increased their consumption capacity. The U.S. by helping to develop Europe/Japan that in turn helps the U.S. in terms of trade with those countries.

Third, this focused expenditure approach will in the short and long terms spur African business development, thus creating millions of jobs for Africans and also creating wealth in the local African economies based on the velocity of money (circulation of money in each local economy). In the longer run, the need for U.S. foreign assistance to Africa will either diminish or vanish. Furthermore, the African Economic Development Revolving Fund will be repaid its investment as the investments in Africa improves Africans' living standards and increase business activities.

Fourth, the various turnkey project(s) such as schools, hospitals, airports and highways and factories will be physically located in those countries in each zone. Therefore, neither a corrupt and heartless President of an African country nor corrupt government officials and employees in those countries will not have the opportunity to steal the <u>cash</u> and deposit the cash in Swiss and other foreign bank accounts.

Furthermore, neither the presidents nor their corrupt government officials and employees can physically move hydroelectric plants, schools, hospitals and/or highways to Switzerland or Paris. A great example is in the early 1960s, the United States funded the construction of the JFK Hospital in Monrovia, Liberia. In almost 50 years, JFK Hospital is the main government hospital in Liberia. The building is still standing because the various corrupt governments that have run Liberia hence have not been able to steal the hospital and move it to Switzerland.

In conclusion, if President Obama implements the foregoing **"Change for Africa,"** it will be dramatic and breathtaking mimicking his fantastic victory. The author submits that the best and only way the United States can have a positive impact on the development of Africa in the 21st Century is by the U.S. asserting direct control over the expenditure of U.S. economic development funding for Africa, not as a hand out or "international welfare", but as a revolving fund available for access based on repayment into the funds to keep it solvent.

Without the Whitehouse asserting direct control and consolidating the economic development of Africa, the Continent of Africa will continue to be plagued by corruption which inevitably leads to civil wars because very few corrupt individuals will continue to control and enjoy the wealth of the various African countries.

Therefore, it is recommended that if any government in any of the four zones refuses this approach to the expenditure of U. S. Economic Development funds for Africa then the U. S. should withhold economic assistance to that country. However, the funds should remain in the Revolving Fund for Africa. Once the refusing and/or corrupt government leaves office, the funds could be made available to be invested as outlined herein and/or as amended.

The author first submitted the foregoing ideas for consideration to President William Jefferson Clinton in 1997. I have attached the exchange of communications between the Whitehouse and the author.

P. NATHANIEL BOE
Attorney-at-Law

October 28, 1996

Honorable William Jefferson Clinton
President, United States of America
The White House
1600 Pennsylvania Avenue
Washington, DC 20500

RE: NEW U.S. 21ˢᵗ CENTURY DEVELOPMENT (MARSHALL) PLAN FOR AFRICA

Dear President Clinton:

First, I thank you very much for announcing last week that the United States of America is taking a leadership role in establishing a RAPID RESPONSE FORCE FOR AFRICA designed to prevent disasters such as the senseless Liberian Civil War which has resulted in the death of over Two Hundred Thousand (200,000) innocent and helpless Liberian men, women and children.

I write to propose a NEW UNITED STATES' 21ˢᵗ CENTURY DEVELOPMENT (MARSHALL) PLAN FOR AFRICA (attached) which both compliments your administration's proposed RAPID RESPONSE FORCE FOR AFRICA and will have an immediate positive impact on the Eight Hundred Million (800,000,000) Africans who live south of the Sahara. The 21ˢᵗ Century Plan for Africa, if implemented, will also eliminate the massive theft of U.S. aid by various corrupt African governments, creates millions of new jobs for Americans and Africans, creates a new huge consumer market for U.S. products, lays the foundations of democracy and diminishes future incidences of civil wars.

I strongly believe that if the proposed 21ˢᵗ Century Plan for Africa is implemented, by the end of your second term, the living standards of Africans living south of the Sahara will have improved by over One Hundred (100) percent. Such an achievement will go down in history with respect to Africans as the greatest for any American President during the 20ᵗʰ Century besides the Civil Rights and Voting Rights Acts of the 1960s. Mr. President, during your first term, the young man from HOPE, Arkansas, brought HOPE back to America by creating millions of new jobs and guiding the U.S. as the sole leader of the world. I hope and pray that you will bring real HOPE to Africa before you retire to HOPE, Arkansas four (4) years from November 5, 1996.

Thank you very much for your attention to this urgent matter.

Respectfully submitted,

P. Nathaniel Boe
Attorney-at-Law

Attachment

208 SOUTH LASALLE STREET, SUITE 705 • CHICAGO, ILLINOIS • 60604
PHONE: (312) 553-4615 • FAX: (312) 553-4656

THE WHITE HOUSE

WASHINGTON

November 6, 1996

Mr. P. Nathaniel Boe
Suite 705
208 South Lasalle Street
Chicago, Illinois 60604

Dear Nathaniel:

Thank you for sharing your views with me.

My Administration remains committed to advancing democracy and human rights, as well as promoting trade, prosperity, regional stability and economic growth in Africa. We have supported democratic transitions in South Africa, Angola, Malawi, Ethiopia, and Mozambique. Additionally, we are helping Africa nurture and sustain its democratic institutions. In fiscal year 1994, we increased our funding for democratic elections and institutions in Africa to $119 million from $5 million the previous year. We plan to continue our support of private groups such as the National Endowment for Democracy and the African Institute, which have played critical roles in promoting democracy.

We have also demonstrated our commitment to advancing democracy and regional growth and prosperity through our financial assistance programs. My Administration bolstered South Africa's transition to democracy with a $600 million multiyear assistance program to meet the urgent need for jobs, housing, health care, basic education, and black private sector development. Working closely with the Southern Africa Development Community, my Administration will also invest $300 million over the next five years to strengthen economic ties, capitalize small businesses, improve transportation and communication, and encourage support for nongovernmental organizations and other advocates of democracy in the region.

During the Cold War, the primary security challenge presented by Africa to the West was the possible spread of communism. With the end of the Cold War, these security challenges have changed. Today, the central security challenge in Africa is internal conflict within national borders. These disputes have the capability of spreading into neighboring countries. In response to this evolving threat, we are strengthening the capacity of regional organizations so they can resolve their own differences. My Administration has already provided $4.5 million to strengthen the Organization of African Unity's Mechanism for Conflict Prevention, Management, and Resolution.

As we move forward with our many African initiatives, I appreciate your interest.

Sincerely,

Bill Clinton

THE WHITE HOUSE
WASHINGTON

November 7, 1996

Mr. P. Nathaniel Boe
Suite 705
208 South Lasalle Street
Chicago, Illinois 60604

Dear Nathaniel:

Thank you so much for your letter. President Clinton greatly appreciates the trust and confidence you have shown in him by writing.

To ensure that your concerns are addressed, I am forwarding your letter to the Department of State for review and any appropriate action. Please bear in mind that it may take some time to look thoroughly into the issues you have raised. Should you wish to contact the Department of State directly, you may write to: Department of State, 2201 C Street, N.W., Washington, D.C. 20520.

Many thanks for your patience.

Sincerely,

James A. Dorskind
Special Assistant to the President
Director of Correspondence and
Presidential Messages

United States Department of State

Washington, D.C. 20520

December 3, 1996

P. Nathaniel Boe
Attorney-at-Law
208 South LaSalle Stree, Suite 705
Chicago, IL 60604

Dear Mr. Boe:

Your letter of September 30 was directed to my office by
the President's staff. It was good to hear of your interest in
the welfare of the underdeveloped countries in Africa. In your
"Marshall Plan for Africa," you outlined a strategy intended to
help African citizens attain higher living standards while
creating new jobs for U.S. citizens. Those are two of the U.S.
government's primary foreign policy goals in Africa.

In an effort to achieve these and other important
objectives, the State Department's Africa Bureau supports the
retention of development assistance programs, especially those
administered by the U.S. Agency for International Development
(USAID). With the decline in U.S. foreign aid, however, Africa
received less than $670 million in Development Assistance and
$14 million in Economic Support Funds for Fiscal Year 1997.

These funds must support a wide array of programs to
improve African living conditions in areas such as health,
environment, and education. USAID also sponsors humanitarian
programs to prevent and mitigate natural and man-made
disasters. In addition, U.S. foreign assistance is used to
promote democracy, good governance and economic reform, three
of the most critical strategies for boosting Africa's economic
and social development. One of the lessons we have learned is
that foreign assistance is most effective when programs are
conducted in these areas simultenously, over a number of years,
so they can complement one another.

I have enclosed some materials published by USAID on
development planning and assistance policy that you might find
useful. Thank you again for your correspondance.

Sincerely,

Joseph Saloom
Director
Economic Policy Staff

Attachments

Developing Africa from Within

Africa is a vastly and fabulously rich continent. Based on information in the public domain, Africa has more natural resources than several continents combined. BUT the ordinary Peoples of Africa are among the world's poorest.

This paradox exists because the powerful nations of the world have not been serious to help Africa to develop from within. They see Africa as rather the source of raw materials and do not care for the people who live in Africa. Additionally, the powerful nations of the world provide safe havens for various thoughtless African despots who commit despicable and heinous crimes against their own people then run to the powerful nations to rest or plan their next evils against their own African people. These African leaders intentionally chose to kill or starve their own people rather than use the funds from the natural resources to feed or develop their countries.

Another stupidity of some African leaders is they steal the funds from the natural resources of their countries and deposit them in the banks of the powerful nations. They then turn around and borrow the same money from those same banks on behalf of their countries at unbelievable interest rates. The same African leaders then steal the loan proceeds thus leaving their countries destitute.

Beginning on January 20, 2009, President Obama has the power to begin to "Change" the disaster that exists in Africa over the past 1000 years.

My fervent prayer is that Almighty God will give President Obama the courage and strength to issue an Executive Order pursuant to his executive powers to "conduct foreign affairs" to wit:

- Ban entry into the United States any African leader (public or private sector) and their subordinates who kill, command or support the killing of their own people.

- Deport to their country of origin any African whether U.S. citizens or permanent residents who plan, support or participate in bringing war upon their people then run away to the United States.

- Ban all African government leaders, their families, friends and business associates from opening bank accounts in the United States or acquiring properties in the United States. Let them bank and invest their money in their home countries.

- Ban medical treatments to African government leaders and their families so that they can use the resources of their countries to build first class medical facilities in their home countries. Certain African countries could be exempted if the U.S. Department of Health and Human Services advises the President that the government leaders of that country have provided adequate medical facilities for their home countries.

- Require American companies doing business in Africa to follow the Biblical edict to treat Africans (Americans' neighbors on this earth) as the Americans would like to be treated themselves. Those American businesses should inculcate a Fairness Doctrine in their business transactions with Africans and help to develop Africa rather than take the natural resources of Africa and leave the ordinary citizens of Africa destitute.

In conclusion, I strongly believe that the United States of America is a wonderful country and with President Obama's leadership, America can set the Continent of Africa on an irreversible path to development. The rest of the world will follow America's lead. With God above, President Obama can change Africa. As President Obama said during the campaign "this is our moment, this is our time" to help Change Africa. **"Yes We Can!"**

CHANGING THE WORLD

President Barack Obama's election has changed the world in the most profound way. That is the United States will not only open its door to the oppressed and downtrodden, but America will redouble its efforts as the chief advocate for justice, peace, development and prosperity for all mankind wherever they live.

With His Excellency Barack Obama as the President of the United States of America, America will reclaim its role as the pre-eminent country in the world with the moral authority to change the misfortunes of the world's poorest.

As you may be aware, most of the countries whose citizens are poor are very wealthy countries with abundant natural resources. But, published reports indicate that the wealth does not reach the vast majority of their citizens who are destitute.

America must be seen as the chief advocate for the poor masses in their countries. One strategic approach to help the billions of poor people throughout the world is for the United States to work with the leaderships of those countries where the United States gets raw materials from to establish a mechanism whereby the people who sit directly on the raw materials get direct benefits from those resources.

As is the case most often than not, the leaders of some countries hate themselves, hate the citizens of their own countries and rather kill their own citizens than provide them with food, shelter, clothing, safe drinking water, electricity, education, healthcare and roads.

President Obama should make it as a condition for American companies doing business in any foreign country to take raw materials from any country that government must sign an agreement to use the proceeds to develop that country and not kill their own people as a way to keep them silent about corruption.

Like the Sullivan Principles successfully used in South Africa that helped to end apartheid, the United States of America should adopt the "President Barack Obama Principles" that will change the world in the most positive way. Because the citizens of the world will perceive the United States of America as being on their side and their chief advocate for positive "Change" in the world.

Mr. President, if you can persuade the leaders of the world to do the right things for their own people, you will not only change America, but you will actually positively change the world forever!

Chapter 6
America, Oh America,
Land of Unlimited
Opportunities

The United Stated of America is a wonderful country because in America all things are possible. President Obama could not have made his "improbable journey" from a childhood filled with challenges to an adult life on the South side of Chicago, moving unto the United States Senate then to Presidency of the Great United States of America.

Many men and women who preceded the present generation of Americans made the ultimate sacrifices with their lives. As discussed in Smiles of our Forefathers, President Abraham Lincoln and Rev. Dr. Martin Luther King, Jr. are two of the most prominent Americans who sacrificed their lives to make the United States of America a wonderful country.

President Barack Obama as a visionary leader foresaw that the American People were ready for change. So, President Barack Obama used one word **"Change"** to transform the universe in the most positive way unimaginable.

So let it be written for the ages that at High Noon on January 20, 2009, America and the world will never be the same.

President Barack Obama, may God bless you and guide the work of your hands. May God continue to bless the Great United States of America!!!!!!!!!!! !!!!!!!!!!!!!!

THANK YOU

My sincerest gratitude to my Great Father Mr. Moses G. Boe the late Superstar Preacher for the African Gospel League Church. I thank my mother Mrs. Trandleh T. Boe for her love and prayers over the years.

I thank my lifetime partner and lovely wife Mrs. Sylvia T. Boe for her immense help with this book especially her invaluable critique of this book. I also thank my children for their support and encouragement.

As I wrote this book over the past 60 days, there were many days of sleepless nights. I almost postponed the publication date. But several of my friends and business associates encouraged me not to postpone what I could do today, because the book may just help one person and that will make it a successful book.

Finally, I thank all my family members, relatives, friends and business associates for their patience with me.

About the Author

P. **Nathaniel Boe, Esq.** is an Attorney and Counselor-at-Law practicing corporate, contracts, commercial and real estate law in Chicago, Illinois, USA, and has concluded contracts and commercial transactions in excess of **US $3 Billion Dollars**. Cllr. Boe also provides consulting services in the areas of strategic planning, federally funded contract administration and procurement. Cllr. Boe currently manages over **US$60 Million Dollars** of real estate projects on behalf of one of his clients. Cllr. Boe is also the Legal Counsel for an engagement with an annual budget of **US$175 Million Dollars**

Cllr. Boe is the President and CEO of several businesses including Boe Group, Inc., Liberian Investment, Inc., Liberian International Services, Inc., NSB Properties and New Millionaires Investment Fund, LLC.

Cllr. Boe was born on October 13, 1960 in Sayon's Town, Wharzon, #3 District, Grand Bassa County, Republic of Liberia, and his parents are Mr. Moses G. Boe and Mrs. Trandleh Boe. He has five brothers namely Amos Boe, Zell D. Boe, Abraham G. S. Boe, W. Sampson D. Boe and Elijah L. Boe and two sisters namely Marnelo Boe and Jurdo Boe.

Cllr. Boe began his formal education at the age of eleven (11), was homeless in Monrovia for four (4) years and was student Council President and Valedictorian of his 1981 Assemblies of God High School graduating class. Cllr Boe earned a Bachelor of Science degree in Economics in 1988 from Chicago State University and graduated from the University of Iowa College of Law with a **Doctor of Jurisprudence (JD) degree** in 1991. Cllr. Boe is admitted to practice law in the State of Illinois and U.S. Federal District Courts (1991) and the Republic of Liberia (1998).

Cllr. Boe and his beautiful wife, Sylvia T. Boe, and son, P. Nathaniel Boe, Jr., reside in Chicago, Illinois. Cllr. and Mrs. Boe have two daughters, Youjay Green of Rhode Island, USA and Konah Jalloh of Monrovia, Liberia.

Cllr. Boe is the chairman and general counsel of the Foundation for Peace and Stability in Liberia, Inc. The foundation provides humanitarian assistance to Liberians in the Republic of Liberia.

P. Nathaniel Boe is a published author of the book titled **_Miracle on the Atlantic Coast, How to Transform Liberia into a Peaceful and Prosperous Country._ This is the premier "how to do book" for the development of Liberia and Africa as a whole.** The book is available worldwide on the internet and at Cllr. Boe's official website: www.pnateboe.com